SIDE BY SIDE

English Through Guided Conversations
2A

Steven J. Molinsky

Bill Bliss

Illustrated by

Richard E. Hill

Prentice-Hall Inc., Englewood Cliffs, New Jersey 07632

Library of Congress Cataloging in Publication Data

MOLINSKY, STEVEN J.
    Side by Side

    Includes indexes.
        1. English language—Conversation and phrase books.
2. English language—Text books for foreign speakers.
I. Bliss, Bill. II. Title.
PE1131.M58 1983   428.3′4   82-20425
ISBN 0-13-809772-0 (Book 2A)

Printed in the United States of America

10

Editorial/production supervisor: Penelope Linskey
Art/camera copy supervisor: Diane Heckler-Koromhas
Cover design by Suzanne Behnke
Manufacturing buyer: Harry P. Baisley

0-13-809772-0

PRENTICE-HALL INTERNATIONAL, INC., *London*
PRENTICE-HALL OF AUSTRALIA PTY. LIMITED, *Sydney*
EDITORA PRENTICE-HALL DO BRASIL, LTDA., *Rio de Janeiro*
PRENTICE-HALL OF CANADA, LTD., *Toronto*
PRENTICE-HALL OF INDIA PRIVATE LIMITED, *New Delhi*
PRENTICE-HALL OF JAPAN, INC., *Tokyo*
PRENTICE-HALL OF SOUTHEAST ASIA PTE. LTD., *Singapore*
WHITEHALL BOOKS LIMITED, WELLINGTON, *New Zealand*

Contents

BOOK **2A**

To the Teacher

Side by Side: Book Two is a conversational grammar book.

We do not seek to describe the language, nor prescribe its rules. Rather, we aim to help students learn to *use* the language grammatically, through practice with meaningful conversational exchanges.

This book is intended for adult and young-adult learners of English. It is designed to provide the intermediate-level student with the basic foundation of English grammar, through a carefully sequenced progression of conversational exercises and activities.

WHY A CONVERSATIONAL GRAMMAR BOOK?

Grammar is usually isolated and drilled through a variety of traditional structure exercises such as repetition, substitution, and transformation drills. Such exercises effectively highlight particular grammatical structures . . . but they are usually presented as a string of single sentences, not related to each other in any unifying, relevant context.

Traditional dialogues, on the other hand, may do a fine job of providing examples of real speech . . . but they don't usually offer sufficient practice with the structures being taught. Teachers and students are often frustrated by the lack of a clear grammatical focus in these meaningful contexts. Furthermore, it's hard to figure out what to *do* with a dialogue after you've read it, memorized it, or talked about it.

In this book we have attempted to combine the best features of traditional grammatical drills and contextually rich dialogues. The aim is to actively engage the students in meaningful conversational exchanges within carefully structured grammatical frameworks. The students are then encouraged to break away from the textbook and *use* these frameworks to create conversations *on their own*.

GRAMMATICAL PARADIGMS

Each lesson in the book covers one or more specific grammatical structures. A new structure appears first in the form of a grammatical paradigm, a simple schema of the structure.

These paradigms are to be a reference point for students as they proceed through the lesson's conversational activities. While these paradigms highlight the structures being taught, they are not intended to be goals in themselves.

We don't want our students simply to parrot back these rules: we want them to engage in conversations that show they can *use* them correctly.

GUIDED CONVERSATIONS

Guided Conversations are the dialogues and question-and-answer exchanges which are the primary learning devices in this book. Students are presented with a model conversation that highlights a specific aspect of the grammar. In the exercises that follow the model, students pair up and work "side by side," placing new content into the given conversational framework.

How to Introduce Guided Conversations

There are many ways to introduce these conversations. We don't want to dictate any particular method. Rather, we encourage you to develop strategies that are compatible with your own teaching style, the specific needs of your students, and the particular grammar and content of the lesson at hand.

Some teachers will want books closed at this stage, giving their students a chance to listen to the model before seeing it in print.

Other teachers will want students to have their books open for the model conversation or see it written on the blackboard. The teacher may read or act out the conversation while students follow along, or may read through the model with another student, or may have two students present the model to the class.

Whether books are open or closed, students should have ample opportunity to understand and practice the model before attempting the exercises that follow it.

How to Use Guided Conversations

In these conversational exercises, the students are asked to place new content into the grammatical and contextual framework of the model. The numbered exercises provide the student with new information which is "plugged into" the framework of the model conversation. Sometimes this framework actually appears as a "skeletal dialogue" in the text. Other times the student simply inserts the new information into the model that has just been practiced. (Teachers who have written the model conversation on the blackboard can create the skeletal dialogue by erasing the words that are replaced in the exercises.)

The teacher's key function is to pair up students for "side by side" conversational practice and then to serve as a resource to the class: for help with the structure, new vocabulary, and pronunciation.

"Side by side" practice can take many forms. Most teachers prefer to call on two students at a time to present a conversation to the class. Other teachers have their students pair up and practice the conversations together. Or small groups of students might work together, pairing up within these groups and presenting the conversations to each other.

This paired practice helps teachers address the varying levels of ability of their students. Some teachers like to pair stronger students with weaker ones. The slower student clearly gains through this pairing, while the more advanced student also strengthens his or her abilities by lending assistance to the speaking partner.

Other teachers will want to pair up or group students of *similar* levels of ability. In this arrangement, the teacher can devote greater attention to students who need it while giving more capable students the chance to learn from and assist each other.

While these exercises are intended for practice in conversation, teachers also find them useful as *writing* drills which reinforce oral practice and enable students to study more carefully the grammar highlighted in the conversations.

Once again, we encourage you to develop strategies that are most appropriate for your class.

The "Life Cycle" of a Guided Conversation

It might be helpful to define the different stages in the "life cycle" of a guided conversation.

I. *The Presentation Stage:*
The model conversation is introduced and is practiced by the class.

II. *The Rehearsal Stage:*
Immediately after practicing the model, students do the conversational exercises that follow it. For homework, they practice these conversations, and perhaps write out a few. Some lessons also ask students to create their own original conversations based on the model.

III. *The Performance Stage:*
The next day students do the conversational exercises in class, preferably with their textbooks and notebooks closed. Students shouldn't have to memorize these conversations. They will most likely remember them after sufficient practice in class and at home.

IV. The Incorporation Stage:
   The class reviews the conversation or reviews pieces of the conversation in the days that follow. With repetition and time, the guided conversation "dissolves" and its components are incorporated into the student's active language.

ON YOUR OWN

An important component of each lesson is the On Your Own activity. These student-centered exercises reinforce the grammatical structures of the lesson while breaking away from the text and allowing students to contribute content of their own.

These activities take various forms: role-plays, extended guided conversations, questions about the student's real world, and topics for classroom discussion and debate. In these exercises the students are asked to bring new content to the classroom, based on their interests, their backgrounds, and the farthest reaches of their imaginations.

We recommend that the teacher read through these activities in class and assign them as homework for presentation the next day. In this way, students will automatically review the previous day's grammar while contributing new and inventive content of their own.

On Your Own activities are meant for simultaneous grammar reinforcement and vocabulary building. Students should be encouraged to use a dictionary when preparing these exercises. Thus, they will use not only the words they know, but the words they would *like* to know in order to bring their own interests, backgrounds, and imaginations into the classroom. As a result, students will be teaching each other new vocabulary and also sharing a bit of their lives with others in the class.

In conclusion, we have attempted to make the study of English grammar a lively and relevant experience for the student. While conveying to you the substance of our textbook, we hope that we have also conveyed the spirit: that learning the grammar can be conversational . . . student-centered . . . and fun.

Steven J. Molinsky
Bill Bliss

Review:
Simple Present Tense
Present Continuous Tense
Subject Pronouns
Object Pronouns
Possessive Adjectives

I am	I'm
He	He's
She } is	She's }
It	It's
→	eating.
We	We're
You } are	You're }
They	They're

Am I	
	he
Is } she	
	it
	eating?
	we
Are } you	
	they

	I am.
	he
	she } is.
	it
Yes,	
	we
	you } are.
	they

Read and practice.

A. Are you busy?

B. Yes, I am. I'm studying.

A. What are you studying?

B. I'm studying English.

Complete these conversations using the model above.

1. Is Helen busy?
cooking spaghetti

2. Is Tom busy?
reading the newspaper

3. Are Bobby and Judy busy?
studying mathematics

4. Are you busy?
typing a letter

5. Are you and your brother busy?
cleaning the basement

6. Is Jane busy?
knitting a sweater

7. Are Mr. and Mrs. Watson busy?
baking cookies

8. Is Beethoven busy?
composing a new symphony

9. Is Whistler busy?
painting a portrait of his mother

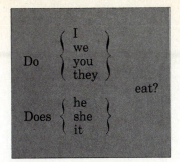

$$\left.\begin{array}{l}\text{I}\\\text{We}\\\text{You}\\\text{They}\end{array}\right\} \text{eat.}$$

$$\left.\begin{array}{l}\text{He}\\\text{She}\\\text{It}\end{array}\right\} \text{eats.}$$

$$\text{Do} \left\{\begin{array}{l}\text{I}\\\text{we}\\\text{you}\\\text{they}\end{array}\right\} \text{eat?}$$

$$\text{Does} \left\{\begin{array}{l}\text{he}\\\text{she}\\\text{it}\end{array}\right\}$$

$$\text{Yes,} \left\{\begin{array}{l}\text{I}\\\text{we}\\\text{you}\\\text{they}\end{array}\right\} \text{do.}$$

$$\left\{\begin{array}{l}\text{he}\\\text{she}\\\text{it}\end{array}\right\} \text{does.}$$

A. What are you doing?

B. I'm practicing the piano.

A. Do you practice the piano very often?

B. Yes, I do. I practice the piano whenever I can.

1. What's Edward doing?
bake bread

2. What's Janet doing?
swim

3. What are Mr. and Mrs. Green doing?
exercise

4. What are you doing?
read Shakespeare

5. What are you and your friend doing?
study English

6. What's Mary doing?
write to her grandparents

7. What's your neighbor doing?
play baseball with his son

8. What are Mr. and Mrs. Baker doing?
meditate

9.

No,
$$\left\{\begin{array}{l} I \\ we \\ you \\ they \end{array}\right\}$$
don't. (do not)

$$\left\{\begin{array}{l} he \\ she \\ it \end{array}\right\}$$
doesn't. (does not)

No, I'm not. (am not)

$$\left\{\begin{array}{l} he \\ she \\ it \end{array}\right\}$$
isn't. (is not)

$$\left\{\begin{array}{l} we \\ you \\ they \end{array}\right\}$$
aren't. (are not)

A. Do you like to ski?

B. No, I don't.
I'm not a very good skier.

1. Does Jim like to dance?
dancer

2. Does Rita like to sing?
singer

3. Do Mr. and Mrs. Brown like to skate?
skaters

4. Do you like to type?
typist

5. Do you and your friend like to play tennis?
tennis players

6. Does Shirley like to swim?
swimmer

7. Does David like to study?
student

8. Do you like to play sports?
athlete

I	my	me
he	his	him
she	her	her
it	its	it
we	our	us
you	your	you
they	their	them

A. Who are you calling?

B. **I'm** calling **my** brother in Chicago.

A. How often do you call **him**?

B. I call **him** every Sunday evening.*

A. What are George and Herman talking about?

B. **They're** talking about **their** grandchildren.

A. How often do they talk about **them**?

B. They talk about **them** all the time.*

*You can also say:
every day, week, weekend, month, year
every morning, afternoon, evening, night
every Sunday, Monday, . . . January, February, . . .

once a
twice a
three times a ⎫
four times a ⎬ day, week, month, year
· ⎭
·
·

all the time

1. Who is Mrs. Lopez calling?
daughter in San Francisco

2. Who are you writing to?
uncle

3. Who is Walter visiting?
neighbors across the street

4. Who is Mrs. Morgan writing to?
son in the army

5. Who is Mr. Davis arguing with?
landlord

6. What are the students complaining about?
homework

7. What are you complaining about?
electric bill

8. Who is Mr. Crabapple shouting at?
employees

9. Who is Little Red Riding Hood visiting?
grandmother

10.

1. Tell the class about yourself. Answer these questions and then ask other students:

Where are you from?
Where do you live now?
What do you do? (I'm a mechanic, a student . . .)
Where do you work/study?

2. Talk about the people in your family and ask other students about their families:

Are you married?   single?
Do you live with your parents?   Do you live alone?

3. Tell the class about your _____ (husband, wife, children, parents, brother(s), sister(s) . . .):

What are their names?
How old are they?
Where do they live?
What do they do?   Where?

4. Tell the class about your interests and ask other students about theirs:

Do you like to play sports?   cards?   chess? . . .?
How often do you go swimming?   play cards?   play chess? . . .?
What else do you like to do in your free time?

Review:
Simple Past Tense
(Regular and Irregular Verbs)
Past Continuous Tense

What did I he she it we you they do?	I He She It We You They worked.	I He She It was We You They were tired.

Read and practice.

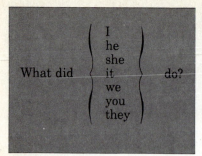

A. Did Henry sleep well last night?

B. Yes, he did. He was VERY tired.

A. Why? What did he do yesterday?

B. He **cleaned his apartment** all day.

1. *you*
study English

2. *Gloria*
work hard

3. *David and Jeff*
wash windows

4. *Miss Henderson*
teach

5. *Mr. and Mrs. Warren*
look for an apartment

6. *Jack*
ride his bicycle

7. *Irene*
write letters

8. *The President*
meet important people

9. _____

I He She It We You They	did/didn't (did not)

I He She It	was/wasn't (was not)
We You They	were/weren't (were not)

A. Did Barney smoke a lot before his job interview?

B. Yes, he did. He was nervous.

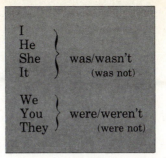

A. Did Helen do well on her English exam?

B. No, she didn't. She wasn't prepared.

1. Did Marylou cry a lot when her dog ran away?
Yes, _____ upset.

2. Did Katherine sleep well last night?
No, _____ tired.

3. Did you fall asleep during the lecture?
Yes, _____ bored.

4. Did Mr. and Mrs. Mason finish their dinner last night?
No, _____ hungry.

5. Did the football coach shout at his players after they lost the game?
Yes, _____ angry.

6. Did they have anything to drink after dinner last night?
No, _____ thirsty.

7. Did Tommy cover his eyes during the science fiction movie?
Yes, _____ scared.

8. Did George and his brother leave on the two o'clock train?
No, _____ on time.

I
He
She
It
} was

working.

We
You
They
} were

A. How did John break his arm?

B. He broke it while he was **playing tennis**.

1. How did Sally break her leg?
ski down a mountain

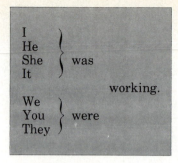

2. How did Martin lose his wallet?
play baseball with his son

3. How did Peggy meet her husband?
read in the library one day

4. How did Mr. and Mrs. Thompson burn themselves?
bake cookies

5. How did Walter cut himself?
shave

6. How did Alan get a black eye?
argue with his neighbor

7. How did Martha cut herself?
prepare dinner

8. How did Rita rip her pants?
dance in a discotheque

9. How did Fred meet his wife?
wait for the bus one day

10. How did Presto the Magician hurt himself?
practice a new magic trick

ON YOUR OWN

Talk with other students in your class:
Do you remember how you met your (husband, wife, boyfriend, girlfriend, best friend)?

Where were you?
What were you doing?
What was he/she doing?

TELL ME ABOUT YOUR VACATION

1. Did you go to Paris?
   No, we didn't.
   Where did you go?
   We went to Rome.

2. Did you get there by boat?
   No, _____.
   How _____?
   _____ by plane.

3. Did your plane leave on time?
   No, _____.
   How late _____?
   _____ two hours late.

4. Did you have good weather during the flight?
   No, _____.
   What kind of _____?
   _____ terrible weather.

5. Did you stay in a big hotel?
   No, _____.
   What kind of _____?
   _____ a small hotel.

6. Did you eat in fancy restaurants?
   No, _____.
   Where _____?
   _____ cheap restaurants.

7. Did you speak Italian?
No, _____.
What language _____?
_____ English.

8. Did you take many photographs?
No, _____.
How many _____?
_____ just a few photographs.

9. Did you buy any clothing?
No, _____.
What _____?
_____ souvenirs.

10. Did you swim in the Mediterranean?
No, _____.
Where _____?
_____ in the pool at our hotel.

11. Did you see the Colosseum?
No, _____.
What _____?
_____ the Vatican.

12. Did you travel around the city by taxi?
No, _____.
How _____?
_____ by bus.

13. Did you send postcards to your friends?

No, _____.

Who _____?

_____ our relatives.

14. Did you write to them about the monuments?

No, _____.

What _____?

_____ the weather.

15. Did you meet a lot of Italians?

No, _____.

Who _____?

_____ a lot of other tourists.

16. Did you come home by plane?

No, _____.

How _____?

_____ by boat.

ON YOUR OWN

Did you take a trip this year? Did you travel to another city?
Did you visit a friend or a relative out of town?
Talk with other students in your class about your last trip:

Where did you go?
How did you get there?
Where did you stay?
What did you do there?
How long were you there?
Did you have a good time?

If you have some photographs of your last trip, bring them to
class and talk about them with the other students.

Review:
   Future: Going to
   Future: Will
   Future Continuous Tense
   Possessive Pronouns

I	am	
He She It	is	going to read.
We You They	are	

What am I going to do?

Where is he going to live?

Who are they going to call?

Expressions of Time

yesterday this tomorrow	morning, afternoon, evening	last night tonight tomorrow night

last this next	week, month, year, Sunday, Monday, . . . spring, summer, . . . January, February, . . .

Read and practice.

A. Are you going to plant carrots this year?

B. No, I'm not. I planted carrots LAST year.

A. What are you going to plant?

B. I'm going to plant tomatoes.

1. Is Ted going to wear his blue suit today?
his black suit

2. Is Barbara going to cook fish tonight?
chicken

3. Are you and your family going to go to Europe this summer?
Mexico

4. Is Charlie going to play popular music this evening?
jazz

5. Are you going to give your brother a watch for his birthday this year?
a tie

6. Are Mr. and Mrs. Peterson going to watch the football game on Channel 2 this Monday night?
the movie on Channel 4

7. Is Professor Hawkins going to teach European History this semester?
American History

8. Are you going to take ballet lessons this year?
tap dance lessons

9. Is Mrs. McCarthy going to buy grapes this week?
bananas

10. Are you going to call the landlord this time?
the plumber

I	will	I'll		
He	will	He'll		
She	will	She'll		
It	will →	It'll	} work.	
We	will	We'll		
You	will	You'll		
They	will	They'll		

I	
He	
She	
It	won't work.
We	(will not)
You	
They	

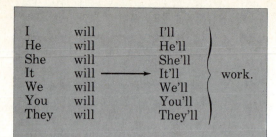

A. Will Richard get out of the hospital soon?

B. Yes, he will. He'll get out in a few days.

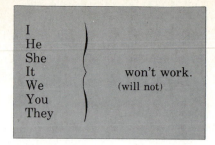

A. Will Sherman get out of the hospital soon?

B. No, he won't. He won't get out for a few weeks.

1. Will the play begin soon?
Yes, _____ at 8:00.

2. Will the game begin soon?
No, _____ until 3:00.

3. Will Bob and Betty see each other again soon?
Yes, _____ this Saturday night.

4. Will John and Julia see each other again soon?
No, _____ until next year.

5. Will the soup be ready soon?
Yes, _____ in a few minutes.

6. Will the turkey be ready soon?
No, _____ for several hours.

7. Will Mom be back soon?
Yes, _____ in a little while.

8. Will Shirley be back soon?
No, _____ for a long time.

I'll He'll She'll It'll We'll You'll They'll	be working.

A. Will you be home this evening?

B. Yes, I will.
I'll be **watching TV**.

A. Will Jane be home this evening?

B. No, she won't.
She'll be **working late at the office**.

1. *Tom*
read

2. *Mr. and Mrs. Harris*
paint their bathroom

3. *you*
swim

4. *Sheila*
do her laundry

5. *you and your family*
ice skate

6. *Sally*
clean her apartment

7. *Mr. and Mrs. Grant*
shop

8. *Donald*
fill out his
income tax form

9. *you*
visit a friend
in the hospital

A TELEPHONE CALL

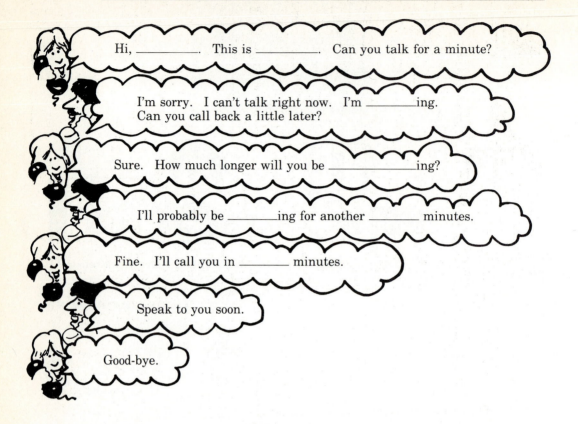

Hi, _____. This is _____. Can you talk for a minute?

I'm sorry. I can't talk right now. I'm _____ing. Can you call back a little later?

Sure. How much longer will you be _____ing?

I'll probably be _____ing for another _____ minutes.

Fine. I'll call you in _____ minutes.

Speak to you soon.

Good-bye.

Complete this conversation and try it with another student in your class.

1. *study English*

2. *do my laundry*

3. *wash my kitchen floor*

4. *help my children with their homework*

5. *have dinner with my family*

6.

I	me	mine
he	him	his
she	her	hers
it	it	its
we	us	ours
you	you	yours
they	them	theirs

A. Could you possibly do me a favor?

B. Sure. I'll be happy to.

A. I've got a problem.
I have to fix my roof and I don't have a ladder.
Could I possibly borrow YOURS?

B. I'm sorry. I'm afraid I don't have one.

A. Do you know anybody who DOES?

B. Yes. You should call Charlie. I'm sure he'll be happy to lend you his.

A. Thank you. I'll call him right away.

A. Could you possibly do me a favor?

B. Sure. I'll be happy to.

A. I've got a problem.
I have to _____ and I don't have a _____.
Could I possibly borrow YOURS?

B. I'm sorry. I'm afraid I don't have one.

A. Do you know anybody who DOES?

B. Yes. You should call _____. I'm sure ____'ll be happy to lend you
_____ (his, hers, theirs).

A. Thank you. I'll call _____ (him, her, them) right away.

1. *fix my TV set*
   screwdriver

2. *fix my front door*
   hammer

3. *write a composition for my English class*
   dictionary

4. *fix my flat tire*
   jack

5. *go to a wedding*
   tuxedo

6.

24

Read and practice.

1.

John is looking forward to this weekend. He isn't going to think about work. He's going to read a few magazines, fix his car, and relax at home with his family.

2.

Alice is looking forward to her birthday. Her sister is going to have a party for her and all her friends are going to be there.

3.

Mr. and Mrs. Williams are looking forward to their summer vacation. They're going to go camping in the mountains. They're going to hike several miles every day, take a lot of pictures, and forget about all their problems at home.

4.

George is looking forward to his retirement. He's going to get up late every morning, visit friends every afternoon, and enjoy quiet evenings at home with his wife.

What are YOU looking forward to? A birthday? A holiday? A day off? Talk about it with other students in your class.

What are you looking forward to?
When is it going to happen?
What are you going to do?

Present Perfect Tense

Read and practice.

A. Are Mr. and Mrs. Smith going to **see** a movie tonight?

B. No, they aren't. They've already **seen** a movie this week.

A. Really? When?

B. They **saw** a movie yesterday.

1. Are Mr. and Mrs. Smith going to eat at a restaurant tonight?
eat–ate–eaten

2. Is Frank going to get a haircut today?
get–got–gotten

3. Is Lucy going to write to her grandmother today?
write–wrote–written

4. Is Bob going to take his children to the zoo today?
take–took–taken

5. Are you going to give blood today?
give–gave–given

6. Are you and your friends going to see a play this evening?
see–saw–seen

7. Is Jennifer going to go to a concert tonight?
go–went–gone

8. Is Philip going to wear his red tie today?
wear–wore–worn

9. Is Mary going to do her laundry today?
do–did–done

10. Is Max going to swim at the health club today?
swim–swam–swum

11. Is Marion going to wash her car today?
wash–washed–washed

12. Is Jim going to bake cookies today?
bake–baked–baked

13. Are you going to buy bananas today?
buy–bought–bought

14. Is Tom going to spend a lot of money at the department store today?
spend–spent–spent

I We You They	} haven't (have not)	
		eaten.*
He She It	} hasn't (has not)	

A. Do you like to swim?

B. Yes, I do.   But I haven't swum in a long time.

A. Why not?

B. I just haven't had the time.

1. Does Kathy like to go to the zoo?

2. Does Robert like to do his English homework?

3. Do you like to read *The New York Times*?

4. Do you and your sister like to bake bread?

5. Do Bob and Sally like to take dance lessons?

6. Does Betsy like to make her own clothes?

7. Does William like to write poetry?

8. Do you like to see your old friends?

9.

*In the present perfect tense the word after **have** or **has** is a past participle. Some past participles (**baked, bought, spent**) are the same as the past tense. Other past participles (**eaten, taken, given**) are different from the past tense. We will tell you when the past participles are different. A list of these words is in the Appendix at the end of the book.

Have	I / we / you / they			eaten?	Yes,	I / we / you / they			have.
Has	he / she / it					he / she / it			has.

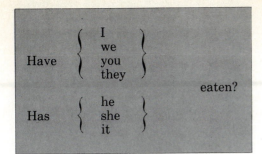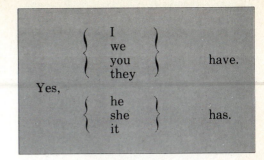

A. Have you **seen** the new Walt Disney movie yet?

B. Yes, I have. I **saw** it yesterday.

1. *you*
write your composition

2. *Nancy*
*ride her new bicycle**

3. *Arthur*
take his driver's test

4. *Sharon and Charles*
do their homework

5. *you*
read Chapter 3

6. *David*
go to the bank

7. *Mr. and Mrs. Chang*
make plans for the
weekend

8. *Stanley*
wear his new suit

9. *you*
meet your new English
teacher

*****ride - rode - ridden**

Have	{ I we you they }	{ }	
			eaten?
Has	{ he she it }	{ }	

No,	{ I we you they }	{ }	haven't.
	{ he she it }	{ }	hasn't.

A. Has Peter left for work yet?

B. No, he hasn't. He has to leave now.

1. *Mildred*
   take her medicine

2. *you*
   finish your homework

3. *Bill*
   get up

4. *John and Julia*
   say good-bye

5. *you*
   feed the dog

6. *Barbara*
   call her boss

7. *Timmy*
   go to bed

8. *you*
   *speak to your landlord**

9. *Harry*
   pay his electric bill

*speak - spoke - spoken

Read and practice.

A. What are you going to do tonight?

B. I'm not sure. I really want to see a good movie. I haven't seen a good movie in a long time.

A. What movie are you going to see?

B. I don't know. Have you seen any good movies recently?

A. Yes, I have. I saw a VERY good movie just last week.

B. Really? What movie did you see?

A. I saw *Gone with the Wind*.

B. And you liked it?

A. I LOVED it! I think it's one of the BEST movies I've ever seen.

A. What are you going to do tonight?

B. I'm not sure. I really want to _____ a good _____.
I haven't _____ a good _____ in a long time.

A. What _____ are you going to _____?

B. I don't know. Have you _____ any good _____s recently?

A. Yes, I have. I _____ a VERY good _____ just last week.

B. Really? What _____ did you _____?

A. I _____ "_____."

B. And you liked it?

A. I LOVED it! I think it's one of the BEST _____s I've ever _____.

1. *see – play*

2. *read – book*

3. *eat at – restaurant*

4. *go to – discotheque**

*Or: nightclub, cafe.

Present Perfect vs.
Present Tense
Present Perfect vs.
Past Tense
For, Since

for	since
three hours	three o'clock
two days	yesterday afternoon
a week	last week
a long time	1960
•	•
•	•
•	•

Read and practice.

A. How long have you known*each other?

B. We've known each other **for two years**.

*know - knew - known

A. How long have you been sick?

B. I've been sick **since last Thursday**.

1. How long have Mr. and Mrs. Jones known each other?
three years

2. How long have Mr. and Mrs. Peterson been married?
1945

3. How long has Tommy liked girls?
last year

4. How long has Diane had problems with her back?
two years

5. How long have you had a headache?
ten o'clock this morning

6. How long has Mrs. Brown been a teacher?
thirteen years

7. How long have there been satellites in space?
1957

8. How long have you owned this car?
five and a half years

9. How long has John owned his own house?
1971

10. How long have you been interested in astronomy?
many years

11. How long has Lucy been interested in computer technology?
a long time

12. How long have you been here?
1963

A. Do you know Mrs. Potter?

B. Yes, I do. I've known her for a long time.

A. How long have you known her?

B. I've known her **since I was a little boy**.

A. Are you two engaged?

B. Yes, we are. We've been engaged for a long time.

A. How long have you been engaged?

B. We've been engaged **since we finished high school**.

1. Does your brother play the piano?
since he was eight years old

2. Is your friend Victor a professional musician?
since he finished college

3. Do you have a fever?
since I got up yesterday morning

4. Does Mary's leg hurt?
since she fell down on the sidewalk last week

5. Are you interested in modern art?
since I read about Picasso

6. Is Jeffrey interested in French history?
since he visited Paris

7. Do you like jazz?
since I was a teenager

8. Do you know how to ski?
since we were very young

9. Does Johnny know how to count to ten?
since he was two years old

10. Is your brother married?
since he got out of the army

11. Do you want to be an actress?
since I saw "Gone with the Wind"

12. Do your children know about "the birds and the bees"?*
since they were nine years old

*the facts of life.

39

A. Has Ralph always been a carpenter?

B. No, he hasn't.
He's been a carpenter for the last ten years.
Before that, **he was** a painter.

A. Have you always taught history?

B. No, I haven't.
I've taught history since 1970.
Before that, **I taught** geography.

1. Has Fred always been thin?.
the last three years

2. Has Roberta always had short hair?
she finished college

3. Have you always liked classical music?
the past few years

4. Have your parents always been Democrats?
*Watergate**

*an American political scandal in 1973–74.

5. Has Steven always spoken with a Boston accent?
he moved to Boston

6. Have you always had a dog?
the past five or six years

7. Has Andy always wanted to be an astronaut?
last September

8. Has Louis always been the store manager?
the last six months

9. Has Janet always known all the people in her apartment building?
the fire last year

10. Has Larry always owned a sports car?
he won the lottery

Answer these questions and then ask other students in your class.

1. What is your present address?
How long have you lived there?
2. What was your last address?
How long did you live there?

3. Who is the President/Prime Minister of your country?
How long has he/she been the President/Prime Minister?
4. Who was the last President/Prime Minister of your country?
How long was he/she the President/Prime Minister?

5. Who is your English teacher now?
How long has he/she been your English teacher?
6. Who was your last English teacher?
How long was he/she your English teacher?

Read and practice.

IT'S BEEN A LONG TIME

A. George!

B. Tony! I can't believe it's you! I haven't seen you in years.

A. That's right, George. It's been a long time. How have you been?

B. Fine. And how about YOU?

A. Everything's fine with me, too.

B. Tell me, Tony. Do you still live on Main Street?

A. No. I haven't lived on Main Street for several years.

B. Where do you live NOW?

A. I live on River Road. And how about YOU? Do you still live on Central Avenue?

B. No. I haven't lived on Central Avenue since 1975.

A. Where do you live NOW?

B. I live on Park Boulevard.

A. Tell me, George. Are you still a barber?

B. No. I haven't been a barber for several years.

A. Really? What do you do NOW?

B. I'm a taxi driver. And how about YOU? Are you still a painter?

A. No. I haven't been a painter for a long time.

B. Really? What do you do NOW?

A. I'm a carpenter.

B. Tell me, Tony. Do you still play the violin?

A. No. I haven't played the violin for many years. And how about YOU? Do you still go fishing on Saturday mornings?

B. No. I haven't gone fishing on Saturday mornings since I got married.

A. Well, George. I'm afraid I have to go now. We should get together soon.

B. Good idea, Tony. It's been a long time.

Pretend that it's ten or fifteen years from now. You're walking along the street and suddenly you meet a student who was in your English class. Try this conversation. Remember, you haven't seen this person for ten or fifteen years.

A. _____!

B. _____! I can't believe it's you! I haven't seen you in years.

A. That's right, _____. It's been a long time. How have you been?

B. Fine. And how about YOU?

A. Everything's fine with me, too.

B. Tell me, _____. Do you still live on _____?

A. No. I haven't lived on _____ (for/since) _____.

B. Where do you live NOW?

A. I live on _____. And how about YOU? Do you still live on _____?

B. No. I haven't lived on _____ (for/since) _____.

A. Where do you live NOW?

B. I live on _____.

A. Tell me, _____. Are you still a _____?

B. No. I haven't been a _____ (for/since) _____.

A. Really? What do you do NOW?

B. I'm a _____. And how about YOU? Are you still a _____?

A. No. I haven't been a _____ (for/since) _____.

B. Really? What do you do NOW?

A. I'm a _____.

B. Tell me, _____. Do you still _____?

A. No. I haven't _____ (for/since) _____. And how about YOU? Do you still _____?

B. No. I haven't _____ (for/since) _____.

A. Well, _____. I'm afraid I have to go now. We should get together soon.

B. Good idea, _____. It's been a long time.

Present Perfect
Continuous Tense

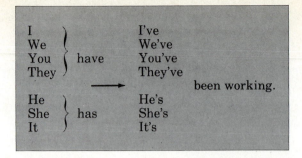

I We You They	} have	→	I've We've You've They've
He She It	} has		He's She's It's

been working.

Read and practice.

A. How long have you been waiting?

B. I've been waiting for two hours.

A. How long has Henry been working at the post office?

B. He's been working at the post office since 1957.

1. How long have you been feeling bad?
yesterday morning

2. How long has Nancy been playing the piano?
several years

3. How long has the phone been ringing?
five minutes

4. How long have Mr. and Mrs. Brown been living on Appleton Street?
1948

5. How long has Maria been studying English?
ten months

6. How long has Frank been going out with Sally?
three and a half years

7. How long have you been having problems with your back?
high school

8. How long have we been driving?
seven hours

9. How long has it been snowing?
late last night

10. How long has your baby son been crying?
early this morning

11. How long have they been building the new bridge?
two years

12. How long has Arnold been lying in the sun?
twelve noon

$$\text{Have} \begin{Bmatrix} \text{I} \\ \text{we} \\ \text{you} \\ \text{they} \end{Bmatrix} \text{been working?}$$

$$\text{Has} \begin{Bmatrix} \text{he} \\ \text{she} \\ \text{it} \end{Bmatrix}$$

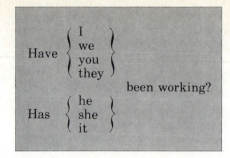

A. What are your neighbors doing?

B. They're arguing.

A. Have they been arguing for a long time?

B. Yes, they have. They've been arguing all day.*

*You can also say: all morning, all afternoon, all evening, all night.

1. *you
studying*

2. *Robert
ironing*

3. *Laura
waiting for the bus*

4. *you and your friends
standing in line for
concert tickets*

5. *Ricky
talking to his girlfriend*

6. *Jane
looking for her keys*

7. *Mr. and Mrs. Wilson
washing their windows*

8. *your car
making strange noises*

9.

A. You look tired.* What have you been doing?

B. I've been writing letters since ten o'clock this morning.

A. Really? How many letters have you written?

B. Believe it or not, I've already written fifteen letters.

A. Fifteen letters?! NO WONDER you're tired!

A. Mary looks tired.* What has she been doing?

B. She's been baking cakes since nine o'clock this morning.

A. Really? How many cakes has she baked?

B. Believe it or not, she's already baked seven cakes.

A. Seven cakes?! NO WONDER she's tired!

*You can also say: exhausted.

1. *you*
wash windows

2. *Dr. Anderson*
see patients

3. *Miss Shultz*
give piano lessons

4. *Mr. and Mrs. Johnson*
buy Christmas presents

5. *you*
pick apples

6. *Mr. Williams*
plant flowers

7. *your grandmother*
mend socks

8. *Bob*
take photographs

9. *you and your friends*
review our English lessons

10. *Jennifer*
write thank-you notes

11. *John*
go to job interviews

12. *you*
fill out income tax forms

A. I'm nervous.

B. Why?*

A. I'm going to **fly in an airplane** tomorrow, and I've never **flown in an airplane** before.

B. Don't worry! I've been **flying in airplanes** for years. And believe me, there's nothing to be nervous about!

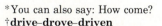

1. *buy a used car*

2. *have a party*

3. *drive† downtown*

4. *go to a job interview*

5. *give blood*

6. *take a karate lesson*

*You can also say: How come?
†**drive–drove–driven**

7. *speak at a meeting*

8. *teach an English class*

9. *run*in a marathon*

10. *sing† in front of an audience*

11. *ask for a raise*

12.

Answer these questions and ask other students in your class.

1. Have you ever flown in an airplane?
(Where did you go?)

2. Have you ever been in the hospital?
(Why were you there?)

3. Have you ever met a famous person?
(Who did you meet?)

4. Have you ever been very embarrassed?
(What happened?)

5. Have you ever been in an accident?
(What happened?)

6. _____?

7. _____?

*run–ran–run
†sing–sang–sung

Complete this conversation and act it out with another student in your class.

AT THE DOCTOR'S OFFICE

A. How are you feeling, (Mr./Mrs./Miss/Ms.) _____?

B. Well, Doctor. I've been having problems with my _____.

A. I'm sorry to hear that. How long have you been having problems with your _____?

B. (For/Since)_____.

A. Have you ever had problems with your _____ before?

B. No. Never. This is the first time.

A. Tell me, (Mr./Mrs./Miss/Ms.) _____. Have you been sleeping O.K.?

B. No, Doctor. I haven't had a good night's sleep since my _____ began to bother me.

A. And how about your appetite? Have you been eating well lately?

B. { Yes, I have. }
{ No, I haven't. }

A. What have you been eating?

B. I've been eating _____
_____.

(after the examination)

A. Well, (Mr./Mrs./Miss/Ms.) _____. I think you should _____.*

B. Do you think that will help?

A. Yes, indeed. A lot of people have been coming to me lately with _____ problems, and I've been advising all of them to _____.

B. Thank you, Doctor. You've been a great help.

A. It's been a pleasure, (Mr./Mrs./Miss/Ms.) _____. I'm sure you'll be feeling better soon.

*take aspirin three times a day; exercise more; drink a lot of water; rest in bed for a few days; see a specialist;...

7

Gerunds
Infinitives
Review: Present Perfect and
Present Perfect Continuous
Tenses

to read	reading
to dance	dancing
to swim	swimming

Read and practice.

A. Do you **like to watch TV**?

B. Yes. I **enjoy watching TV** very much.
Watching TV is my favorite way to relax.

1. *you*
listen to music

2. *Tom*
swim

3. *Lucy*
read

4. *you and your friends*
dance

5. *Mr. and Mrs. Green*
play tennis

6. *you*
ice skate

7. *Shirley*
sew

8. *Alan*
play chess

9. *your parents*
go to the movies

like to work	can't stand to work |*	—
like working	can't stand working	avoid working

A. Does Ronald **like** { **to travel** / **traveling** } by plane?

B. No. He **can't stand** { **to travel** / **traveling** } by plane.

He **avoids traveling** by plane whenever he can.

1. *Sally*
do her homework

2. *Mr. and Mrs. Simon*
drive downtown

3. *you*
talk on the telephone

4. *Jim*
work late at the office

5. *you and your friends*
talk about politics

6. *Julie*
eat spinach

7. *you*
practice the piano

8. *Michael*
visit his mother-in-law

9. *Mr. and Mrs. Kendall*
play cards with their
neighbors

Ask another student: What do you enjoy doing?
What do you avoid doing whenever you can?

---

*You can also say:
{ **hate to** work }
{ **hate** working }

A. How did you **learn to swim** so well?

B. I **started** { **to swim** / **swimming** } when I was young, and I've been **swimming** ever since.

A. I envy you. I've never **swum** before.

B. I'll be glad to teach you how.

A. Thank you.* But isn't **swimming** very difficult?

B. Not at all. After you **practice swimming** a few times, you'll probably **swim** as well as I do.

*You can also say: I appreciate that. That's very kind of you. That's very nice of you.

A. How did you learn to _____ so well?

B. I started { to _____ / _____ing } when I was young, and I've been _____ing ever since.

A. I envy you. I've never _____ before.

B. I'll be glad to teach you how.

A. Thank you.* But isn't _____ing very difficult?

B. Not at all. After you practice _____ing a few times, you'll probably _____ as well as I do.

1. *draw†*

2. *ski*

3. *figure skate*

4. *bake bread*

5. *tap dance*

6. *play chess*

7. *box*

8.

*You can also say: I appreciate that. That's very kind of you. That's very nice of you.
†**draw–drew–drawn**

59

A. Guess what I've decided to do!

B. I can't guess.   What?

A. I've **decided to get married**.

B. You HAVE?   That's GREAT!
How long have you been **thinking about getting married**?

A. For a long time, actually.
I **considered getting married** YEARS ago, but I never did.

B. Why have you **decided to get married** NOW?

A. I've decided that if I don't **get married** now, I never will.
Do you think I'm making the right decision?

B. Yes, I do.   I think **getting married** is a WONDERFUL idea!

A. I'm glad you think so.

A. Guess what I've decided to do!

B. I can't guess. What?

A. I've decided to _____.

B. You HAVE? That's GREAT!
How long have you been thinking about _____ing?

A. For a long time, actually.
I considered _____ing YEARS ago, but I never did.

B. Why have you decided to _____ NOW?

A. I've decided that if I don't _____ now, I never will.
Do you think I'm making the right decision?

B. Yes, I do. I think _____ing is a WONDERFUL idea!

A. I'm glad you think so.

1. *move to Chicago*

2. *buy a new car*

3. *get a dog*

4. *go on a diet*

5. *grow a beard**

6. *go back to college*

7. *start my own business*

8.

***grow–grew–grown**

{ **start to** eat **start** eating }	{ **continue to** eat **continue** eating }	{ — **stop** eating }
{ **begin to** eat **begin** eating }	{ — **keep on** eating }	{ — **quit** eating }

Complete this conversation and try it with another student in your class.

A. I have some good news!

B. What is it?

A. I've decided to stop* _____ing.

B. That's GREAT! Do you really think you'll be able to do it?

A. I think so. But it won't be easy.
I've been _____ing for a long time.

B. Have you ever tried to stop _____ing before?

A. Yes. Many times. But every time I've stopped _____ing,
I've started† { to_____
 _____ing } again after a few days.

B. I hope you'll be successful this time.

A. I hope so, too.
After all, I can't keep on‡ _____ing for the rest of my life!

1. *smoke* **2.** *gamble* **3.** *eat junk food* **4.**

*You can also say: quit.
†You can also say: **begin–began–begun.**
‡You can also say: continue.

Past Perfect Tense
Past Perfect Continuous Tense

I
He
She
It
We
You
They
} had eaten.

Read and practice.

the weekend before

A. Did Mr. and Mrs. Jones **drive** to the beach last weekend?

B. No. They didn't want to.
They **had** just **driven** to the beach the weekend before.

the night before

1. Did Mr. and Mrs. Henderson see a movie last Saturday night?

the evening before

2. Did George eat at a restaurant yesterday evening?

the week before

3. Did Rosa take a day off last week?

the weekend before

4. Did you go skiing last weekend?

the Sunday before

the night before

5. Did you and your friends have a picnic last Sunday?

6. Did Shirley have pizza for dinner last night?

the year before

the weekend before

7. Did Gregory take a geography course last year?

8. Did Helen give a party last weekend?

the evening before

the day before

9. Did Mr. and Mrs. Stevens discuss politics at the dinner table yesterday evening?

10. Did you go window-shopping last Saturday?

the week before

the day before

11. Did Mabel bake one of her delicious apple pies last week?

12. Did Philip wear his polka dot shirt to work last Tuesday?

the weekend before

13. Did Stanley do magic tricks for his friends last weekend?

14.

A. Did you get to the **plane** on time?

B. No, I didn't.
By the time I got to the **plane**, it had already **taken off**.

1. concert
   begin

2. post office
   close

3. train
   leave

4. lecture
   end

5. movie
   start

6. meeting
   finish

7. bank
   close

8. boat
   sail away

9. parade
   go by

| I He She It We You They | hadn't eaten. (had not) |

A. Did George enjoy **seeing his old friends** last night?

B. Yes, he did. He hadn't **seen his old friends** in a long time.

1. Did you enjoy swimming in the ocean last weekend?

2. Did Janice enjoy singing with the choir last Sunday?

3. Did Mr. and Mrs. Gleason enjoy taking a walk along the beach yesterday?

4. Did you and your friends enjoy going out for dinner last night?

5. Did Susan enjoy visiting her grandparents last Sunday afternoon?

6. Did Andrew and Eric enjoy having chocolate cake for dessert last night?

7. Did Professor Nelson enjoy seeing his former students last week?

8. Did Walter enjoy playing "hide and seek" with his children last night?

9. Did Mrs. Thompson enjoy reading her old love letters last weekend?

A. Have you heard about Harry?

B. No, I haven't. What happened?

A. He broke his leg last week.

B. That's terrible! How did he do that?

A. He was playing soccer . . . and he had never played soccer before.

B. Poor Harry! I hope he feels better soon.

A. Have you heard about _____?

B. No, I haven't. What happened?

A. (He/She) _____ last week.

B. That's terrible! How did (he/she) do that?

A. (He/She) was _____ing . . . and (he/she) had never _____ before.

B. Poor _____! I hope (he/she) feels better soon.

Tom

Doris

1. _twist his ankle_
   fly* a kite

2. _sprain her wrist_
   play tennis

*fly–flew–flown

3. *burn himself*
bake chocolate chip cookies

4. *get hurt in an accident*
ride on a motorcycle

5. *get a black eye*
box

6. *injure her knee*
wrestle

7. *break his front teeth*
chew on a steak bone

8. *lose her voice*
sing opera

9. *sprain his back*
do the tango

10.

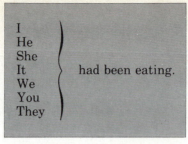

I
He
She
It
We
You
They
} had been eating.

A. I heard that Arnold failed his driver's test last week.
Is it true?

B. Yes, it is . . . and it's really a shame.
He had been practicing for a long time.

A. I heard that _____ last week.
Is it true?

B. Yes, it is . . . and it's really a shame.
(He/She/They) had been _____ing for a long time.

I heard that . . .

1. Lucy lost her job at the bank
work there

2. Boris lost the chess match
practice

3. Ted and Carol broke up
   go together

4. Robert did poorly on his English examination
   study for it

5. Sally had to cancel her trip to Canada
   plan it

6. Dick and Janet cancelled their wedding
   plan to get married

7. Mrs. Gold had another heart attack
   feel better

8. Mr. and Mrs. Hardy moved
   live in this neighborhood

9. Lisa got sick and couldn't see the parade
   hope to see it

10. Roger caught a cold and couldn't go camping
    look forward to it

Read and practice.

1.

Patty had planned to have a party last weekend. She had been getting ready for the party for a long time. She had invited all of her friends. She had cooked lots of food. And she had cleaned her apartment from top to bottom. But at the last minute, she got sick and had to cancel her party. Poor Patty! She was really disappointed.

2.

Michael had planned to ask his boss for a raise last week. He had been preparing to ask his boss for a raise for a long time. He had come to work early for several weeks. He had worked late at the office every night. And he had even bought a new suit to wear to the appointment with his boss. Unfortunately, before Michael could even ask for a raise, his boss fired him.

3.

John and Julia had planned to get married last month. They had been planning their wedding for several months, and all of their friends and relatives had been looking forward to the ceremony. Julia had bought a beautiful wedding gown. John had rented a fancy tuxedo. And they had sent invitations to 150 people. But at the last minute, John "got cold feet"* and they had to cancel the wedding.

Talk with other students in your class about plans YOU had that "fell through":

What had you planned to do?
How long had you been planning to do it?
What had you done beforehand?
What went wrong? (What happened?)
Were you upset? disappointed?

*You can also say: got scared.

Two-Word Verbs:
Separable
Inseparable

SEPARABLE TWO-WORD VERBS

bring back the book   **bring** it **back**
call up Sally   **call** her **up**
put on your boots   **put** them **on**

Read and practice.

A. When is the repairman going to **bring back** your television?

B. He's going to **bring** it **back** sometime next week.

1. When are you going to **call up** your cousin in Chicago?

2. When is John going to **fill out** his income tax form?

3. When is Greta going to **pick up** her clothes at the cleaner's?

4. When is Maria going to **pick out** her wedding gown?

5. When are you going to **put away** your winter clothes?

6. When is Peter going to **bring back** his library books?

7. When is your landlord going to **turn on** the heat?

8. When is Margaret going to **throw out** her old magazines?

9. When are you going to **hang up** your new portrait?

> { **put on** your boots }
> { **put** your boots **on** } **put** them **on**

A. Did you remember to { **turn off** the oven / **turn** the oven **off** } ?

B. Oh, no! I completely forgot!
I'll **turn** it **off** right away.

1. *bring back*
your library books

2. *put away*
your toys

3. *call up*
your Aunt Gertrude

4. *fill out*
your income tax form

5. *hand in*
your English homework

6. *take out*
the garbage

7. *take off*
your boots

8. *put on*
your raincoat

9. *turn on*
the "no smoking" sign

A. Do you think I should keep these old love letters?

B. No, I don't.*
I think you should **throw** them **away**.

*You can also say: No, I don't think so. Not really. That probably isn't a very good idea.

1. *keep my ex-boyfriend's
ring
give back*

2. *leave the air-conditioner
on
turn off*

3. *hand my homework in
do over*

4. *erase all my mistakes
cross out*

5. *throw out this old milk
use up*

6. *try to remember Sally's
telephone number
write down*

7. *make my decision
right away
think over*

8. *accept my new job offer
turn down*

9. *ask the teacher the defi-
nition of this new word
look up*

Read and practice.

Hi, Paul. This it Tom.
Would you like to get together today?

I'm afraid I can't.
I have to **fill out** my income tax form.

Are you free after you **fill** it **out**?

I'm afraid not.
I also have to **bring** my library books **back**.

Would you like to get together after you **bring** them **back**?

I'd really like to, but I can't.
I ALSO have to **pick** my sister **up** at the airport.

You're really busy today!
What do you have to do after you **pick** her **up**?

Nothing. But by then I'll probably be EXHAUSTED!
Let's get together tomorrow instead.

Fine. I'll call you in the morning.

Speak to you then.

A. Hi, _____. This is _____.
Would you like to get together today?

B. I'm afraid I can't.
I have to _____.

A. Are you free after you _____?

B. I'm afraid not.
I also have to _____.

A. Would you like to get together after you _____?

B. I'd really like to, but I can't.
I ALSO have to _____.

A. You're really busy today!
What do you have to do after you _____?

B. Nothing. But by then I'll probably be EXHAUSTED!
Let's get together tomorrow instead.

A. Fine. I'll call you in the morning.

B. Speak to you then.

1.

2.

☑ clean up my room

☑ put away my clothes

☑ do over my Algebra homework

3.

☑ take down my Christmas decorations

☑ hang up my New Year's party decorations

☑ drop off my suit at the cleaner's

4.

☑ figure out my hospital bill

☑ fill out my insurance form

☑ call up the doctor

Using any of the two-word verbs in this chapter, try this conversation with another student in your class.

5.

☑ _____

☑ _____

☑ _____

INSEPARABLE TWO-WORD VERBS

call on John	call on him
~~call John on~~	~~call him on~~

A. Have you **heard from** your Uncle George recently?

B. Yes, I have. As a matter of fact, I **heard from** him just last week.*

*You can also say: the other day, a few days ago, a few minutes ago . .

1. Have you **heard from** your cousin Betty recently?

2. Have you **looked through** your old English book recently?

3. Have you **run into** Mr. Smith recently?

4. Have you **gotten over** the flu yet?

5. Has your English teacher **called on** you recently?

6. Have you been **picking on** your little brother lately?

TALK ABOUT SOME OF THE PEOPLE IN YOUR LIFE

Answer these questions and then ask other students in your class.

1. Do you have a good friend in another city? Who is he/she? How often do you **hear from** him/her? How long have you known each other?
2. Who do you **get along with** very well? Why?
3. Who do you **take after**? How?
4. Who do you **look up to**? Why?

Complete this conversation and act it out with another student in your class.

IN THE DEPARTMENT STORE

A. May I help you?

B. Yes, please. I'm **looking for** a _____.

A. What size do you wear?

B. I'm not sure. I think I take a size _____.

A. Here's a nice size _____. How do you like (it/them)?

B. I think (it's/they're) a little too _____.*
Do you have any _____s that are a little _____er?*

A. Yes. We have a wide selection.
Why don't you **look through** all of our _____s on your own and **pick out** the (one/ones) you like.

B. Can I **try** (it/them) **on**?

A. Of course. You can **try** (it/them) **on** $\begin{cases} \text{right here.} \\ \text{in the dressing room} \\ \text{over there.} \end{cases}$

*
fancy–plain (dull)
dark–light

(5 minutes later)

A. Well, how $\left(\begin{array}{c}\text{does it}\\\text{do they}\end{array}\right)$ fit?

B. I'm afraid (it's/they're) a little too _____.*
Do you have any _____s that are a little _____er?*

A. Yes, we do. I think you'll like (THIS/THESE) _____.
(It's/They're) a little _____er than the one(s) you just **tried on**.

B. Will you **take** (it/them) **back** if I decide to return (it/them)?

A. Of course. No problem at all. Just **bring** (it/them) **back** within _____
days, and we'll **give** you your money **back**.

B. Fine. I think I'll take (it/them). How much $\left(\begin{array}{c}\text{does it}\\\text{do they}\end{array}\right)$ cost?

A. The usual price is _____ dollars. But you're in luck!
We're having a sale this week, and all of our _____s are _____ percent off
the regular price.

B. That's a real bargain! I'm glad I decided to buy (a) _____ this week.
Thank you so much for your help.

A. It's been my pleasure. Please come again.

*

large	–	small
long	–	short
wide	–	narrow
tight	–	loose (baggy)

1. *raincoat*   **2.** *pair of gloves*   **3.** *sweater*   **4.**

Connectors:
And . . . Too
And . . . Either
So, But, Neither

A. I'm hungry.	A. I'm not hungry.
B. { I am, too. / So am I. }	B. { I'm not either. / Neither am I. }
A. I can swim.	A. I can't swim.
B. { I can, too. / So can I. }	B. { I can't either. / Neither can I. }
A. I have a car.	A. I don't have a car.
B. { I do, too. / So do I. }	B. { I don't either. / Neither do I. }
A. I worked yesterday.	A. I didn't work yesterday.
B. { I did, too. / So did I. }	B. { I didn't either. / Neither did I. }
A. I've seen that movie.	A. I haven't seen that movie.
B. { I have, too. / So have I. }	B. { I haven't either. / Neither have I. }

Read and practice.

A. I'm allergic to cats.

B. What a coincidence!
{ I am, too. / So am I. }

A. I wasn't very athletic when I was younger.

B. What a coincidence!
{ I wasn't either. / Neither was I. }

1. I'm a vegetarian.

2. I didn't see the stop sign.

3. I like strawberry ice cream.

4. I don't like war movies.

5. I can speak four languages fluently.

6. I just lost my job.

7. I'm not a very good tennis player.

8. I'll be on vacation next week.

9. I can't sing very well.

10. I've been feeling tired lately.

11. I have to work late at the office tonight.

12. I won't be able to go bowling next Monday night.

13. I don't drink coffee any more.

14. I forgot to take my clothes off the clothes line this morning.

15. I've never kissed anyone before.

16. I'm a little nervous about this operation.

17. I haven't prepared for today's lesson.

18.

I'm tired, { and he is, too. / and so is he. }

He was angry, { and they were, too. / and so were they. }

They work hard, { and she does, too. / and so does she. }

She studied yesterday, { and I did, too. / and so did I. }

A. Why can't you or the children help me with the dishes?

B. I have to study, { **and they do, too.** / **and so do they.** }

1. A. Why are you and your brother so tired?
B. I stayed up late last night, _____.

2. A. What are you and your girlfriend going to do tomorrow?
B. I'm going to study at the library, _____.

3. A. Why are you and Gloria so nervous?
B. She has an English exam tomorrow, _____.

4. A. Where were you and your husband when the accident happened?
B. I was standing on the corner, _____.

5. **A.** Why can't you or Dr. Johnson see me next Monday?
   B. I'll be out of town, _____.

6. **A.** Why haven't you and your sister been in school for the past few days?
   B. I've been sick, _____.

7. **A.** How do you know Mr. and Mrs. Jenkins?
   B. They sing in the church choir, _____.

8. **A.** Could you or your friend help me bring these packages upstairs?
   B. I'll be glad to help you, _____.

9. **A.** Why don't you or your neighbors complain about this broken door?
   B. I've already spoken to the landlord, _____.

10. **A.** How did you meet your wife?
   B. I was washing clothes at the laundromat one day, _____.

11. **A.** Why are you and your cats hiding under the bed?
   B. I'm afraid of thunder and lightning, _____.

12. **A.** What are you two arguing about?
   B. He wants this parking space, _____.

13. **A.** Why are you and Peter so angry at each other?
   B. I wore a Superman costume to the masquerade party, _____.

14. **A.** Why are you in love with Robert?
   B. I appreciate literature, music, and other beautiful things, _____.

I'm not tired, { and he isn't either.
                and neither is he. }

He wasn't angry, { and they weren't either.
                   and neither were they. }

They don't work hard, { and she doesn't either.
                        and neither does she. }

She didn't study yesterday, { and I didn't either.
                              and neither did I. }

A. Why do you and your husband want to enroll in my dance class?

B. I can't dance the cha cha or the fox trot,
{ **and he can't either.**
  and neither can he. }

1. A. Why do you and William look so confused?
B. I don't understand today's grammar, _____.

2. A. Why didn't you or your parents answer the telephone all weekend?
B. I wasn't home, _____.

3. A. Why do you and your roommate have to move?
B. He didn't have enough money to pay the rent this month, _____.

4. A. Why do you and your sister look so frightened?
B. I've never been on a roller coaster before, _____.

5. **A.** Why are you and your friends so late?
   B. I couldn't remember your address, _____.

6. **A.** What do you and Fred want to talk to me about?
   B. I won't be able to come to work tomorrow, _____.

7. **A.** Why don't you and your friends want to come to the ballgame?
   B. They aren't very interested in baseball, _____.

8. **A.** Why does the school nurse want to see us?
   B. I haven't had a flu shot yet, _____.

9. **A.** What are you and your sister arguing about?
   B. She doesn't want to take the garbage out, _____.

10. **A.** Why didn't you or Mom wake us up on time this morning?
    B. I didn't hear the alarm clock, _____.

11. **A.** Why are you and your husband so quiet this evening?
    B. I'm not very comfortable at big parties, _____.

12. **A.** Why were you and your wife so nervous during the flight?
    B. I had never flown before today, _____.

13. **A.** Why have you and your friends stopped shopping at my store?
    B. I can't afford your prices, _____.

14. **A.** Why don't you and your little sister want me to read *Little Red Riding Hood*?
    B. I don't like fairy tales very much, _____.

> I don't sing, but my sister does.
> He can play chess, but I can't.
> We're ready, but they aren't.
> She didn't know the answer, but I did.

A. Do you know the answer to question number 9?

B. No I don't, but **Charles** does. Why don't you ask him?

1. Do you have a hammer?
my upstairs neighbors

2. Are you interested in seeing a movie tonight?
Bob

3. Can you baby-sit for us tomorrow night?
my sister

4. Have you heard tomorrow's weather forecast?
my father

5. Did you write down the homework assignment?
Maria

6. Do you want to go dancing tonight?
Julia

7. Have you by any chance found a brown and white dog?
the people across the street

8. Were you paying attention when the salesman explained how to put together this toy?
the children

Read and practice.

MY BROTHER AND I

In many ways, my brother and I are exactly the same:
    I'm tall and thin, and he is, too.
    I have brown eyes and black curly hair, and so does he.
    I work in an office downtown, and he does, too.
    I'm not married yet, and neither is he.
    I went to college in Boston, and so did he.
    I wasn't a very good student, and he wasn't either.

And in many ways, my brother and I are very different:
    I like classical music, but he doesn't.
    He enjoys sports, but I don't.
    I've never traveled overseas, but he has.
    He's never been to New York, but I have many times.
    He's very outgoing and popular, but I'm not.
    I'm very quiet and philosophical, but he isn't.

Yes, in many ways, my brother and I are exactly the same.
And in many ways, we're very different. But most important of all,
we like and respect each other. And we're friends.

ON YOUR OWN

Compare yourself with somebody you are close to: a friend,
a classmate, or somebody in your family.

In many ways, _____ and I are exactly the same:

_____

_____

_____

And in many ways, _____ and I are very different:

_____

_____

_____

APPENDIX

Irregular Verbs

Irregular Verbs

be	was	been
become	became	become
begin	began	begun
bite	bit	bitten
blow	blew	blown
break	broke	broken
bring	brought	brought
build	built	built
buy	bought	bought
catch	caught	caught
choose	chose	chosen
come	came	come
cost	cost	cost
cut	cut	cut
do	did	done
draw	drew	drawn
drink	drank	drunk
drive	drove	driven
eat	ate	eaten
fall	fell	fallen
feed	fed	fed
feel	felt	felt
fight	fought	fought
find	found	found
fit	fit	fit
fly	flew	flown
forget	forgot	forgotten
forgive	forgave	forgiven
freeze	froze	frozen
get	got	gotten
give	gave	given
go	went	gone
grow	grew	grown
hang	hung	hung

have	had	had
hear	heard	heard
hide	hid	hidden
hit	hit	hit
hold	held	held
hurt	hurt	hurt
keep	kept	kept
know	knew	known
lead	led	led
leave	left	left
lend	lent	lent
let	let	let
light	lit	lit
lose	lost	lost
make	made	made
mean	meant	meant
meet	met	met
put	put	put
quit	quit	quit
read	read	read
ride	rode	ridden
ring	rang	rung
run	ran	run
say	said	said
see	saw	seen
sell	sold	sold
send	sent	sent
set	set	set
sew	sewed	sewed/sewn
shake	shook	shaken
shrink	shrank	shrunk
sing	sang	sung
sit	sat	sat
sleep	slept	slept

speak	spoke	spoken
spend	spent	spent
stand	stood	stood
steal	stole	stolen
sweep	swept	swept
swim	swam	swum
take	took	taken
teach	taught	taught
tell	told	told
think	thought	thought
throw	threw	thrown
understand	understood	understood
wake	woke	woken
wear	wore	worn
win	won	won
wind	wound	wound
write	wrote	written

Index

Word List

The number after each word indicates the page where the word first appears.

(adj) = adjective,   (n) = noun,   (v) = verb

This word list does not include words that first appeared in Books 1A and 1B.

S/

ADULT LEARNING CENTER
STEINWAY BRANCH
ESL

PLEASE CHECK FOR
_____5_____ RECORDS
_____1_____ PAMPHLETS